LOVE
IS
LOUD

LOVE IS

LOUD

How
DIANE NASH
Led the Civil Rights Movement

WRITTEN BY
SANDRA NEIL WALLACE

ILLUSTRATED BY
BRYAN COLLIER

A Paula Wiseman Book
SIMON & SCHUSTER BOOKS FOR YOUNG READERS

New York London Toronto Sydney New Delhi

"The nonviolent movement . . . is based upon
and motivated by love."
—DIANE NASH

SIMON & SCHUSTER BOOKS FOR YOUNG READERS
An imprint of Simon & Schuster Children's Publishing Division
1230 Avenue of the Americas, New York, New York 10020
Text © 2023 by Sandra Neil Wallace
Illustration © 2023 by Bryan Collier
Book design by Laurent Linn © 2023 by Simon & Schuster, Inc.
All rights reserved, including the right of reproduction in whole or in part in any form.
SIMON & SCHUSTER BOOKS FOR YOUNG READERS and related marks are trademarks of Simon & Schuster, Inc.
For information about special discounts for bulk purchases, please contact Simon & Schuster Special Sales
at 1-866-506-1949 or business@simonandschuster.com.
The Simon & Schuster Speakers Bureau can bring authors to your live event. For more information or to book an event,
contact the Simon & Schuster Speakers Bureau at 1-866-248-3049 or visit our website at www.simonspeakers.com.
The text for this book was set in PT Serif.
The illustrations for this book were rendered in watercolor and collage.
Manufactured in China
0124 SCP
2 4 6 8 10 9 7 5 3
Library of Congress Cataloging-in-Publication Data
Names: Wallace, Sandra Neil, author. | Collier, Bryan, illustrator.
Title: Love is loud : how Diane Nash led the Civil Rights Movement / Sandra Neil Wallace ; illustrated by Bryan Collier.
Other titles: How Diane Nash led the Civil Rights Movement
Description: First edition. | New York : Simon & Schuster Books for Young Readers, [2023] | Includes bibliographical references. |
Audience: Ages 4–8 | Audience: Grades 2–3 | Summary: "A picture book biography of Diane Nash, a Civil Rights Movement leader
at the side of Martin Luther King Jr. and John Lewis. Born in 1938 in Chicago, Diane went on to take command of the
Nashville Movement, leading lunch counter sit-ins and peaceful marches. Diane decides to fight not with anger or violence, but with love.
With her strong words of truth and actions, she works to stop segregation"— Provided by publisher.
Identifiers: LCCN 2022007306 (print) | LCCN 2022007307 (ebook) |
ISBN 9781534451032 | ISBN 9781534451049 (ebook)
Subjects: LCSH: Nash, Diane, 1938-–—Juvenile literature. | African American women civil rights workers—Biography—
Juvenile literature. | Civil rights workers—United States—Biography—Juvenile literature. | Civil rights movements—United States—
History—20th century—Juvenile literature. | African Americans—Civil rights—History—20th century—Juvenile literature. |
United States—Race relations—History—20th century—Juvenile literature.
Classification: LCC E185.97.N37 W35 2023 (print) | LCC E185.97.N37 (ebook) | DDC 323.092 [B]—dc23/eng/20220323
LC record available at https://lccn.loc.gov/2022007306
LC ebook record available at https://lccn.loc.gov/2022007307

Photo of Diane Nash at lunch counter © Gerald Holly / File / The Tennessean, The Tennessean
via Imagn Content Services, LLC- USA TODAY NETWORK
Photo of Diane Nash marching © The Tennessean-USA TODAY NETWORK

You arrive in the spring of 1938 on the South Side, when Chicago's leaves unfurl, emerald green like your baby-girl eyes.

CELEBRATION, JUBILATION. Your parents baptize beautiful, honey-brown you, *Diane Judith Nash*.

Their first, Chicago-born, no way they'll raise you down in the segregated South like they were.

True, Chicago has sides, but in your house, your parents don't talk about divides, hoping you know only love.

At first it works, until you're four, and the world war changes everything.

Your dad joins the army, and your mom works all day punching codes into a machine.

So where does that leave you?

FEARFUL, TEARFUL. You miss their company, but Grandmother Bolton from Tennessee showers you with love. Wonderful and wise, she looks into your emerald eyes and gives you gems of wisdom. You are "more precious than all the diamonds in the world," she'd say, stroking your hair. As you grow in the rhythm and glow of her love, you know it must be true.

Your high school includes everyone. It splashes rainbows of color across your classes. In books, you see signs of separation, but you don't feel it. For teenage you, beauty contests are cool, even if charm school won't accept Negroes. **REFUSING** is **CONFUSING**, but you don't let segregation touch you.

Then you move south to Grandmother's Tennessee—
and Fisk University.

Your Nashville friends take you to the fair, where the
air is filled with sticky, sugar smells of cotton candy.

And suddenly you see it up close, between roller
coasters roiling and corn-dog fryers bubble-boiling—

Two signs for bathrooms: WHITE and COLORED.

REST ROOMS

WHITE   COLORED

Cheeks **BURNING** from the heat of **HUMILIATION**,
now you feel the sting of segregation.

Your friends tell you it's always been this way.

They say to go along to get along.

But you won't follow rules if the rules are wrong.

Your grandmother raised you with the rhythm of love,
and it echoes in your heart.

Proud to be beautiful, honey brown.

No way a sign could say that you are less.

DEFIANT, DETERMINED. Tough as candy-apple coating, on the dusty midway that night, you vow to change wrong into right.

Yet everywhere in Nashville's square, signs say, WHITE ONLY and COLORED ONLY.

You can't drink from the same water fountain.

You can't go to the same school.

And you can't eat at a lunch counter.

For you, this is the worst. A burst of **INDIGNATION**.

You are all about love. You don't want to be arrested for eating at a lunch counter. And you will never go along to get along.

So what can you do?

CONFIDENT, COMPASSIONATE. Before class in a church each day, you and a group of students pray and learn about change in a peaceful way.

At first, you don't think it will work. *Can you really end segregation with love?*

You practice sitting at an imaginary lunch counter, calmly ordering food.

You promise not to be rude if someone shoves you off your stool. And if they throw sugar in your hair, that you won't care.

You grow so **STRONG**, so **DETERMINED**, so **CONVINCED** about **LOVE**. As snow swirls above you and paper hearts fill shop windows that February day, you lead the way to Nashville's lunch counters.

Seeing twenty-one-year-old you sit down with your pearls and your books shakes the cooks and the waitress. She breaks plate after plate as you wait to be served.

Inside, you shake too. **HANDS SWEATING**, **NEVER FORGETTING** the danger, the fear of being arrested for ordering a sandwich.

Your family is also afraid. Of what can happen to you over lunch. They worry you've gotten in with the wrong bunch.

But you stay **BRAVE**. You won't cave. Sit-in after sit-in. As hot coffee burns and sugar turns hair white, you focus on love. And when you get arrested for ordering a sandwich, more students fill the seats each week—one hundred, two hundred, three hundred strong!

Then one April morning—a warning. A bomb explodes, loaded with hate because **LOVE** is **WINNING**. Shattered windows **SPINNING**, falling like rain. **TUMBLING**, **RUMBLING** through a city gone ugly.

Luckily, no one is hurt.

But you don't wait for calm. That bomb lights a **FIRE** in you. A burning **DESIRE** in you to meet the mayor face-to-face.

Thousands of Black Americans and white Americans feel the same as you.

So what do you do?

Quietly walking, without any talking, you silently lead six thousand marching feet to the beat of love.

YOUTHFUL, **TRUTHFUL**. "Striding towards freedom," you say. You meet the mayor at the courthouse steps. Bow-tied and mystified, he says there's nothing he can do.

You know it isn't true. Determined to stop that lie, you look him in the eye and ask if he thinks it's wrong for a mother, a sister, or a brother to be judged by their skin color.

The mayor agrees that it's wrong.

ELATION, **INVIGORATION**. Quick as thunder, you wonder, "Do you mean that to include lunch counters?"

Looking you in the eye, the mayor replies, "Yes."

At that moment, love **SCORES**. It **SOARS** as six thousand loving hands roar with applause.

Unstoppable, unblockable, you prove that

Love is fierce.

Love is strong.

Love is loud!

In May, by your twenty-second birthday, Nashville's lunch counters boom to the loving tune of everyone enjoying meals. Black folks and white folks eat side by side. Students and church ladies munch on sandwiches, lunch on hot dogs, sipping cherry sodas. Swirling sugar into coffee.

No traces of mustard thrown on faces.

Because you dare, Nashville's lunch counters finally serve everyone.

The next night, Martin Luther King Jr. congratulates you on winning a glorious fight without raising a fist. He knows that because of you segregation is through in Nashville. "No lie can live forever," he says. "Walk together, children. Don't get weary."

You don't get weary, because the next right thing is around the corner—a sit-in on wheels. In the North, Black riders and white riders board a bus without a fuss for the Freedom Rides.

Traveling south, they sit where they choose and refuse to obey Southern rules—BLACKS TO THE BACK and WHITE WAITING ROOMS. Because the law of the land says everyone is free to sit or stand together in a bus traveling across America.

When a bomb stops their ride, you decide violence won't win.

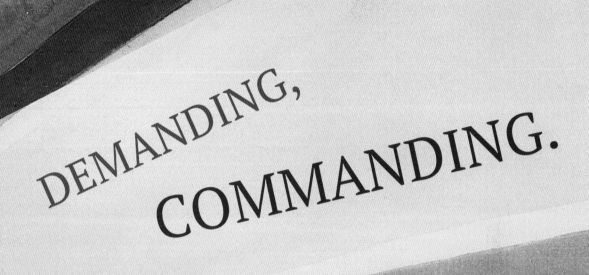

DEMANDING, COMMANDING.

On your twenty-third birthday, you keep freedom riding, with students from Tennessee who want to be on that bus. **NO HIDING. NO FIGHTING BACK** if attacked.

Because of you, the country **WAKES UP**, the president of the United States **SPEAKS UP** and wonders, *Who is Diane Nash?*

A Mississippi judge knows who you are. He charges you with putting Freedom Riders on a bus. For teaching **JUST** and **PEACEFUL, POWERFUL** ways to create change. How is that a crime?

In no time, you march into the courtroom and meet him in the first row, where the judge says only white people go. You don't budge. You're proud! Pregnant with your first baby, no way you'll see your child grow up in the segregated South without a peaceful fight, turning wrong into right.

Grandmother Bolton said you're more precious than diamonds.

But you are afraid. You write a letter to the world that is **HONEST** and **BOLD**.

"I believe that if I go to jail now," you write, "it may help hasten that day when my child and all children will be free."

Like a jolt of electricity, you get the world to see the ugly reality of segregation. Quick as thunder, they wonder, *Will the judge jail a mother-to-be?*

Your sentence is two years! You won't pay bail instead of going to jail. Will your baby be born in prison?

PERSISTING, RESISTING. In jail, it's hard to sleep at night. *Will the cockroaches bite?* As they scurry, you hurry to wash your clothes in the sink.

The judge can't believe you stay in jail for your baby. For freedom. But for you, there is no maybe. JAIL—NO BAIL. The judge doesn't agree, but after ten days, he sets you free.

Unstoppable, unblockable, you prove that

Love is fierce. Love is strong. Love is loud!

In 1963, when freedom marches into Washington, DC, over two hundred thousand marchers fill the monument's square, but you're not there.

The stage is filled with men and Martin Luther King Jr.'s dream. There's no plan for you to stand and have your voice be heard.

ANXIOUSLY, URGENTLY. Only two weeks later, a bomb kills four young girls in a Birmingham church. It hurts so much that you know change must come NOW. But how?

What can you do?

For the first time, you think violence might win. Until you begin to see the next right thing. Because you have a dream too. It's not too late to vote out hate. If thousands of people can march on Washington for freedom, why not in Alabama, where Black people are denied the right to vote?

Thousands of children and grown-ups fill Alabama jails, refusing bail, just like you did in Mississippi, until at last, the Voting Rights Act is passed.

LEADING, PROCEEDING. The following year, your dream is clear. You arrive before spring on the North Side of Vietnam, when bamboo leaves gleam emerald green and bombs fall. You meet that country's president. You greet mothers, sisters, and brothers, babies beautiful, honey brown, and begin talking **PEACE NOT WAR**.

Back home things are different from before. On Chicago's South Side, your mom decides to spread love too, handing out peace pamphlets because of you.
And when the US government takes your passport, there's no way you'll stay quiet.

So what do you do?

RADIANT, MAGNIFICENT. You travel across America for fifty years, so young people will hear how love creates change.

WELCOME, DIANE NASH, the signs say. Wonderful and wise, Diane Nash looks into your eyes and lets you know how she stayed brave the day she got arrested for ordering a sandwich. And why she refused bail and marched to jail to keep freedom rolling. It's because she loved you even before you were born.

SWEETLY, COMPLETELY. Proud to secure every freedom for you, she proved that

Love is fierce.
Love is strong.
Love is loud!

AUTHOR'S NOTE

During the 1960s, Diane Nash was one of the most influential and effective leaders of the Civil Rights Movement, yet most people don't know who she is.

That's because Black women activists faced both racial and gender discrimination. This gender bias also found its way into the movement.

During the March on Washington in 1963, organizers gave the podium microphone to prominent male leaders like Dr. Martin Luther King Jr. and John Lewis. Civil Rights leader Daisy Bates read a pledge to support Dr. King and others in the fight for civil liberties, but none of the women leaders—including Diane Nash—were given the chance to make speeches.

Yet Diane led major campaigns during the civil rights era, all of them creating historic changes to American democracy. Everything Diane led in the fight for change, she won—including integrating Nashville's lunch counters with the Nashville sit-ins, integrating interstate bus travel with the Freedom Rides, and securing voting rights for Black Americans in the South with the passing of the Voting Rights Act. Though she was often afraid, Diane wouldn't be intimidated. She took on mayors and the president of the United States. She stood up to racism and sexism and led the Civil Rights Movement with the power of love.

When Diane moved from Chicago to Nashville in 1959, she was outraged by its segregation laws holding Black people back, including being denied service at lunch counters or in restaurants. She quickly looked for people who were standing up to racism and resisting these laws through nonviolent actions. Diane became part of the Nashville Student Movement that followed the peaceful practices for change attributed to Mohandas Gandhi, known as passive resistance, taught in Nashville by Reverend James Lawson.

But this powerful form of resistance was anything but silent. Soon, Diane led John Lewis and thousands of other nonviolent student protestors in lunch counter sit-ins to integrate Nashville's restaurants. Her courage and discipline laid bare the moral injustice of segregation to millions of Americans who watched the activists on TV being harassed and harmed by white people for simply ordering sandwiches. And it was Diane's confrontation with the mayor that led him to integrate Nashville's lunch counters. "You didn't have to be a man to be courageous," Diane explained.

Putting freedom before education, Diane left university to become a full-time activist after cofounding the national civil rights student organization, the Student Nonviolent Coordinating Committee (SNCC).

When a bomb stopped the Freedom Rides in 1961 and President John F. Kennedy urged the protestors not to continue, Diane refused to let violence overcome. "If we do," she said, "the movement is dead." Diane kept the Freedom Rides running, which led to regulations prohibiting segregation on interstate bus travel. President Kennedy soon recognized Diane as a civil rights leader and asked her to join the committee that helped pass the Civil Rights Act of 1964.

Diane and other activists went to jail to defend their constitutional right to equality, but it was the letter Diane wrote about going to prison for the freedom of her unborn child that shook America. After being released from jail, she helped lead the voting rights campaign in Alabama, and convinced other civil rights leaders, including Dr. King, to march from Selma to Montgomery to publicize how Black people were being denied their constitutional right to vote. "I never saw him as my leader," Diane recalled. "I saw him as being at my side."

Believing that to stop violence and corruption you needed to vote hate out of office, Diane succeeded in helping pass the Voting Rights Act of 1965, ensuring that, like white citizens, all Black citizens needed to do to vote was show ID.

After moving to Chicago in the late 1960s, Diane continued to defend civil rights and women's rights, and to promote peace, not war. "Hating people is not the solution to human problems," she said. Traveling across America for fifty years, she spoke with young people about her activism and how to create change.

"Although we had not yet met you," Diane told them, "we loved you. And we were trying to bring about the best society that we could for you to be born into."

And that's how fierce and strong and loud love is.

ILLUSTRATOR'S NOTE

The story of Diane Nash is one of courage, service, and sacrifice. Painted in watercolor and collage, my art follows Diane as she grows into her maturity and consciousness, surrounded by tremendous love from her parents and grandparents. During the Civil Rights Movement of the 1950s and '60s, in a segregated America, Diane's bravery is on full display as she is determined to end segregation in public places by organizing sit-ins at local lunch counters and Freedom Riders to break down the barriers of segregation of interstate travel on buses in the South. Her life is a testimony that positive change can be made with a strong and powerful love for humankind, and that love must be loud.

Diane Nash integrates the Post House Restaurant lunch counter in Nashville's Greyhound Bus Terminal with university students. (Left to right: Matthew Walker Jr., Peggy Alexander, Diane Nash, and Stanley Hemphill.) March 16, 1960.

TIME LINE

1938—May 15: Diane Judith Nash is born in Chicago, Illinois.

1941–1945: Her parents divorce during World War II. Her dad, Leon Nash, enlists in the US Army. Her mom, Dorothy Bolton, works as a war bonds keypunch operator. Diane's Tennessean grandmother, Carrie Bolton, helps raise her.

1952: Diane attends Hyde Park High School and graduates in 1956.

1953: Diane is denied entry into a Chicago modeling school because she is Black.

1955—January 20: Morgan State University students hold a sit-in and desegregate Read's Drug Store in Baltimore.

1955—March 2: Fifteen-year-old Claudette Colvin refuses to give up her seat to a white person on a Montgomery bus.

1955—November: The Interstate Commerce Commission bans bus segregation across states, but the law is not enforced.

1955–1975: Vietnam War.

1955—December 1: Rosa Parks refuses to give up her seat on a Montgomery bus, fueling the Montgomery Bus Boycott.

1958—August 19: Clara Luper leads successful sit-ins at lunch counters in Oklahoma City, Oklahoma.

1958: Diane enrolls at Howard University in Washington, DC, majoring in English.

1959: She transfers to Fisk University in Nashville, Tennessee.

1959: Outraged at seeing racially segregated bathrooms at the Tennessee State Fair, Diane attends Reverend James Lawson's nonviolent protest workshops at Clark Memorial Methodist Church, where Black and white students learn to challenge segregation through peaceful protests and lunch counter sit-ins.

1960—February 1: North Carolina A & T State University students Joseph McNeil, Franklin McCain, Ezell Blair Jr., and David Richmond sit at a "whites-only" Woolworth's lunch counter, starting the Greensboro sit-ins.

1960—February 13: Diane leads John Lewis and 122 other students to Nashville stores in the first of many lunch counter sit-ins, launching the Nashville Student Movement.

1960—March 16: With students Matthew Walker Jr., Peggy Alexander, and Stanley Hemphill, Diane integrates the Post House Restaurant lunch counter at Nashville's Greyhound Bus Terminal.

1960—April 15: Diane helps start the Student Nonviolent Coordinating Committee (SNCC), encouraged by civil rights leader Ella Baker.

1960—April 19: Civil rights attorney Z. Alexander Looby's Nashville home is bombed. In protest, Diane leads thousands on a silent march to the courthouse and gets mayor Ben West to desegregate the city's lunch counters.

1961—February 6: In solidarity with jailed sit-in students known as the Rock Hill Nine, Diane travels to South Carolina and participates in a lunch counter sit-in. She is arrested and refuses to pay bail, spending thirty days in jail.

1961: Diane leaves Fisk University to focus on civil rights and ending segregation.

1961—May 4: The first Freedom Riders board a Washington, DC, bus to integrate interstate travel.

1961—May 20: With violence threatening to cancel the Freedom Rides, Diane coordinates them from Nashville. The Kennedy administration tries to convince her to stop the rides. She refuses.

1961—November 1: Because of Diane and the Freedom Riders, the Interstate Commerce Commission enforces new regulations to end segregation on buses and transit terminals.

1961: Diane marries civil rights activist James Bevel. They will have two children: Sherrilynn and Douglass. They will divorce in 1968.

1962—April 30: Sentenced to thirty days in a Mississippi jail for coordinating student protests, Diane refuses bail and goes to jail. Pregnant with her first child, she writes a letter to the world about the price of freedom.

1963: Diane helps organize the Birmingham Campaign marches to protest segregation.

1963—July 9: Diane meets President Kennedy. She agrees to join the committee to map out the Civil Rights Act of 1964.

1963—August 28: At the March on Washington, over 200,000 people hear speeches by male civil rights leaders.

1963—September 15: Birmingham's 16th Street Baptist Church is bombed, killing four young girls: Addie Mae Collins, Carol Denise McNair, Carole Robertson, and Cynthia Morris Wesley. Devastated, Diane responds by helping start the Alabama Project and Selma Voting Rights Movement, to vote hate out of office.

1964—July 2: President Johnson signs the Civil Rights Act of 1964 into law. It bans discrimination at businesses and public places based on race, color, religion, sex, or national origin.

1965—August 6: President Johnson signs the 1965 Voting Rights Act to legally end racial discrimination that prevented Black people from voting.

1965: Diane receives the Rosa Parks Award from the Southern Christian Leadership Conference (SCLC).

1966–1967: Diane travels with a group of women peace activists to North Vietnam. She meets with that country's president and North Vietnamese families. When she returns to Chicago, her passport is taken away.

2003: Diane is awarded the Distinguished American Award by the John F. Kennedy Library and Foundation.

2004: She receives the LBJ Award for Leadership in Civil Rights.

2008: The National Civil Rights Museum honors Diane with their Freedom Award.

2009: Diane is awarded an honorary doctorate from Fisk University.

2021: Fisk University's John Lewis Center for Social Justice creates a professorship in Diane's name.

2021—December 21: Nashville's courthouse plaza is named Diane Nash Plaza.

2022—July 7: Diane is awarded the Presidential Medal of Freedom—the highest civilian honor—by President Joe Biden.

LEARN MORE ABOUT DIANE NASH FROM THESE VIDEO INTERVIEWS

Gray DC, *President Biden Honors Diane Nash with Presidential Medal of Freedom*, July 7, 2022. https://www.graydc.com/2022/07/07/president-biden-honors-diane-nash-with-presidential-medal-freedom.

Newsy, *Diane Nash Talks Women and Civil Rights–Era Activism*, February 9, 2016. https://www.youtube.com/watch?v=TaWv4ECln7w.

National Civil Rights Museum, *A Climate of Change: Diane Nash*, 2008. https://www.youtube.com/watch?v=iAG9kABlWaQ.

FOR YOUNG READERS

Perkovich, Olugbemisola Rhuday. *Someday Is Now: Clara Luper and the 1958 Oklahoma City Sit-Ins*. Irvine, CA: Seagrass Press, 2018.

Pinkney, Andrea Davis. *Sit-In: How Four Friends Stood Up by Sitting Down*. New York: Little, Brown Books for Young Readers, 2010.

Powell, Patricia Hruby. *Lift as You Climb: The Story of Ella Baker*. New York: Margaret K. McElderry Books, 2020.

Weatherford, Carole Boston. *Freedom on the Menu: The Greensboro Sit-Ins*. New York: Puffin Books, 2007.

QUOTE SOURCES

Dedication

"The nonviolent movement . . .": Mathew H. Ahmann, ed., *The New Negro*, Notre Dame, IN: Fides Publisher, 1961, p. 43.

"At first it works . . ."

"more precious than . . .": Catherine Ingram, *In the Footsteps of Ghandi,* Berkeley, CA: Prallax Press, 2003, p. 186.

"YOUTHFUL, TRUTHFUL."

"Striding towards freedom.": "NBC White Paper: Sit-In," December 20, 1960, via "Nashville—Confrontation at City Hall: The Civil Rights Act of 1964: A Long Struggle for Freedom," Library of Congress.

"Do you mean that to include . . .": David Halberstam, *The Children,* p. 234.

"Yes": Fred Travis, *Transcribed Dialogue between Mayor Ben West, Diane Nash, and Protestors Regarding Desegregation of Lunch Counters in Nashville, Tennessee,* Fred Travis Papers, 1940–1994, Tennessee State Library and Archives, April 19, 1960.

"The next night . . ."

"No lie can live forever . . .": "King Urges Sit-Ins Continue: Bomb Scare Clears Fisk Gym," *Nashville Banner,* April 21, 1960.

"Grandmother Bolton said . . ."

"I believe that if I go to jail now . . .": Diane Nash letter, April 29, 1962. Carl and Anne Braden papers, University of Tennessee Knoxville Libraries.

Author's Note

"You didn't have to be a man . . .": Barak Goodman, filmmaker, "Diane Nash, Civil Rights Leader," *Makers: Women Who Make America*, PBS Makers documentary series, 2013.

"If we do, the movement . . .": James Farmer, *Lay Bare the Heart*, New York: Arbor House, 1985, p. 203.

"I never saw him as . . .": Barak Goodman, filmmaker, "Diane Nash, Civil Rights Leader," *Makers: Women Who Make America*, PBS Makers documentary series, 2013.

"Hating people is not . . .": Henry Hampton, *Eyes on the Prize: America's Civil Rights Movement 1954–1985.* Boston: Blackside, Inc., 1985, 1988; PBS, 2010.

"Although we had not yet met . . .": Kathryn Flagg, "Civil Rights Leader Diane Nash Recounts Life at the Forefront of Social Change," *Middlebury Newsroom,* April 4, 2018.

SELECTED BIBLIOGRAPHY

Bell, Janet Dewart. *Lighting the Fires of Freedom: African American Women in the Civil Rights Movement*. New York: The New Press, 2018.

Freeman, Sarah Wilkerson, and Beverly Greene Bond, eds. *Tennessee Women: Their Lives and Times—Volume 1*. Athens, Georgia: University of Georgia Press, 2009.

Greenberg, Cheryl Lynn, ed. *A Circle of Trust: Remembering SNCC*. New Brunswick, New Jersey: Rutgers University Press, 1998.

Halberstam, David. *The Children*. New York: Random House, 1998.

Halberstam, David. "Integrate Counters—Mayor." *The Nashville Tennessean*, April 20, 1960.

Hampton, Henry. *Eyes on the Prize: America's Civil Rights Movement 1954–1985*. Boston: Blackside, Inc., 1985, 1988; PBS, 2010.

Hampton, Henry, and Steve Fayer. *Voices of Freedom: An Oral History of the Civil Rights Movement from the 1950s through the 1980s*. New York: Bantam, 1990.

Lartey, Jamiles. "Diane Nash: 'Non-violent Protest Was the Most Important Invention of the 20th Century,'" *Guardian*, April 6, 2017.

Lewis, Andrew B. *The Shadows of Youth: The Remarkable Journey of the Civil Rights Generation*. New York: Hill and Wang, 2009.

Lewis, John, with Michael D'Orso. *Walking with the Wind: A Memoir of the Movement*. New York: Simon & Schuster, 1998.

Mullins, Lisa. *Diane Nash: The Fire of the Civil Rights Movement*. Miami, Florida: Barnhardt & Ashe Publishing, Inc., 2007.

Nash, Diane. "They Are the Ones Who Got Scared." In *Hands on the Freedom Plow: Personal Accounts by Women in SNCC*, edited by Faith S. Holsaert, Martha Prescod Norman Noonan, Judy Richardson, Betty Garman Robinson, Jean Smith Young, and Dorothy M. Zellner, 76–84. Urbana: University of Illinois Press, 2012.

Nelson, Stanley. *Freedom Riders*. Boston: PBS, 2011.

Olson, Lynne. *Freedom's Daughters: The Unsung Heroines of the Civil Rights Movement from 1830 to 1970*. New York: Scribner, 2001.

Talley, James. "Lunch Counter Strikes Hit City." *The Nashville Tennessean*, February 14, 1960.

Wynn, Linda T. "The Dawning of a New Day: The Nashville Sit-Ins, February 13–May 10, 1960." *Tennessee Historical Quarterly* 50, no. 1 (Spring 1991): 42–54.

ACKNOWLEDGMENTS

My sincere thanks to research and digital specialists William B. Eigelsbach and Kyle Hovious, of the Special Collections at the University of Tennessee Knoxville Libraries, for helping me find the letter that Diane Nash wrote to the world before going to prison in Mississippi; archivist Tony Bounds, of the L. Zenobia Coleman Library at Tougaloo College, for Nash family photos; research assistant Meghan Weaver, of the Martin Luther King, Jr. Papers Project at Stanford University, for historic telegrams and letters; Simon & Schuster art director Laurent Linn and illustrator Bryan Collier, for their artistic vision; and to Bryan and editor Paula Wiseman, for encouraging me to write this book.

—S. N. W.

Diane Nash leads three thousand demonstrators on a silent march down Jefferson Street in Nashville to the Metro Courthouse to confront Mayor Ben West on the day of attorney Z. Alexander Looby's house bombing. (Front row, left to right: Rev. C.T. Vivian, Diane Nash, and Bernard LaFayette Jr.) April 19, 1960.